G000277633

BLIND TO UNFAMILIAR FORMS OF LIGHT

Beccy Palmer

Copyright © 2022 by Beccy Palmer.

ISBN-978-1-63767-796-4 (Paperback)
ISBN-978-1-63767-797-1 (eBook)

LCCN: 2022904263

All rights reserved. No part of this book may be reproduced or transmitted in any form or by any means, electronic or mechanical, including photocopying, recording, or by any information storage and retrieval system, without permission in writing from the copyright owner.

The views expressed in this work are solely those of the author and do not necessarily reflect the views of the publisher, and the publisher hereby disclaims any responsibility for them.

All refugees across the world.

Chapter 1

THE REASON

The grandma (Booba) sits on her soft sofa and tells herself that this is it. She has to start to commit to this fully. She thinks about her life, her amazing children, her beautiful grandchildren, her family, her partner, the friends that make the sum of all parts in her life and how she so desperately wants a better world and, yes, now. She smiles. "On your high horse again," she says to herself, and why not? These are unprecedented times as we all keep hearing, but the world and its leaders still move in the same way as though this is the only way. Which brings her onto her book. She giggles as though she's being naughty or maybe acting above her station or experience or skill set. A book, eh?

Ever since she heard this story, it must be decades ago now, she has been haunted by it. We are all confronted at some point in our lives where we have a decision to make, but for most of us that's limited to but no less important than those we see being taken every day by people with little or no understanding of our everyday lives. Again she smiles, "You just can't help yourself, can you?"

Booba suddenly realises that she thinks she's ignored some sort of writing etiquette. Is this a preface, introduction, pre-chapter, chapter one?

She thinks that maybe she could persuade someone with more writing experience to do a preface; sounds good.

The title of the book she got from a science programme where they described very early forms of life that were simply blind to unfamiliar forms of light so either adapted to survive or didn't. It reminded herself of how we are taught, conditioned and sometimes forced into believing that there is only one way to live or die by. That there is a status quo that dictates how we are with each other. Our opinions and judgements are all restricted to a history and way of things that is natural to us, inherent? Booba refuses to believe this. There is or has to be a better way. Human beings are so resourceful, intelligent and, as she has seen so many many times, caring and supporting of others.

Hatred for others because of their colour, religion, race, sexuality or gender is not innate, it's constructed. Constructed by those who would rather we went to war to kill others just like us rather than challenge those who "rule over us". Booba wants to plead with others in such a desperate way, feeling like we all

don't have much time left to reveal our true selves and all the beauty we are capable of as human beings.

Have you ever held your nose and put your head under water in the bath, the swimming pool, the sea? Your eyes closed. You can hear and sense something but it's all much dimmer, more distant, almost not real. Then you come up out of the water, open your eyes and shake your head. It's like suddenly the truth reveals itself.

This is what Booba's book is about. Sometimes the choices we are presented with, however limited, make us who we are and in their own way determine and provoke reactions that could, might, with every hope in Booba's heart, change the course of events and maybe even history and herstory too.

She has done lots of research, reading and hearing about personal accounts during the Holocaust but there are no names in this book, either of people or places, because Booba wants you to imagine it's your city, town, village. To imagine yourself and those you know as the people in the story. This particular recollection is a well told story and still not confirmed as fact or fiction but believable none the less. However, the whole piece is definitely part of Booba's heritage, which she will never tire of retelling.

Chapter 2

ARRIVAL AT
THE CAMP

The night was very warm but slightly damp. It was twilight and the people were gathering outside the theatre, all dressed up, shining, glittering and actually quite beautiful in all their colourful splendour. Definitely glamorous but also a little glowing because of the heat. Small beads of sweat were appearing on people's brows but that didn't matter. Tonight was about trying to forget what was happening, smile, laugh if possible, show affection for others and lend a kind ear to friends. Small groups of people together, chatting, laughing, hearing little stories and recounting their days. The dancer looked out of the window of her green room on the second floor. She loved to people-watch and would get so heavily involved in the small interactions from her window. She would sometimes create a whole life and world around her observations, which she thought was funny, and would shake her head and smile to herself about some of the ridiculous things she would make up. Her dressing room reflected this. There were newspaper cuttings all over the green walls, conveying lots of different stories. Her vast wardrobe of clothes hanging from every possible place or draped across every available space. Flowers in lovely vases at different stages of their lives punctuated the array of garments. She loved this place and her view to the world from her window.

To her amusement and appreciation, the crowd was getting bigger and louder. This was one of the highlights of her week. It could almost feel like things were normal and no one had to fear anything at all.

But just then the men in uniform turned up, laughing as though they owned the very air they all breathed, and everyone stopped as if they did, or needed acceptance or permission to continue. But the uniforms acted as though they didn't even notice or care that their presence created such a reaction; in fact it was exactly the desired reaction.

The dancer at that moment pulled her head back behind her curtain. The fear she felt made her feel dizzy and sick to her stomach, but she fought against this. Telling herself that she wouldn't let them do this to her and it was her space, her art, her world.

The theatre was full, all ages, all people, even the cheap seats were full. The excitement was visible, with lots of chatter and laughter and small screams of "How lovely to see you and looking so well". You could cut the anticipation and excitement with a knife. The lights made it even warmer and created an almost

fantasy-like feel, like a different space, not a theatre but a place where you could forget and just live for that brief moment in time in your own imagination.

The audience became completely absorbed in this occasional world with every act and performance. Soon it was her, the dancer, that would be their main focus. She had done this so many times before but recently had felt that every dance could be her last so would dance as if it were.

The curtain went back, the orchestra started to play and the audience held their breath; it was clearly their favourite part of the evening and she never failed to impress. She knew in different circumstances she would have had so much more choice about her life, her art could have taken her anywhere and her life would have been very different, but now it was her statement of survival.

She entered the stage and danced as though there was no such thing as gravity, time or space. It was captivating, beautiful, glorious. Beads of sweat ran down the sides of her face and she glimpsed her lover in the wings. His face full of pride and so much love it almost overflowed onto the stage.

She was finished and ran, no fell into his arms and at that moment she awoke.

Back in his arms in the cattle carriage of the train. Packed so close it was almost hard to breath and even when you did the air was awful, dusty and full of the smell of the worst things you could imagine.

He stroked her face and kissed her cheek as he held her form in the crowded carriage full of people on a train full of cattle trucks of human beings.

"I think you might have drifted off, my darling," said the lover to the dancer.

"Yes, I think I did, sorry."

"Don't be silly, no need to apologise."

"I was dancing," she said as she snuggled closer to him, her head on the side.

"It must be morning," she commented. She could see rays of sunshine breaking through between the wooden slats like shards of gold shining through the space and suddenly for the first time she could see faces and was overwhelmed. She couldn't do her usual story making nor was it needed as every story was being told through every face and expression of those in the carriage.

The light drew her gaze towards a woman crying and pleading, her face lit up by the light as though she was on stage, in the spotlight.

"I think she's dead, but I don't know," the woman said, sobbing and looking desperate for an answer. "She won't get up and I keep treading on her and I think it must hurt. I feel terrible about it." She looked alone, although surrounded and pushed tightly against others.

The dancer imagined what it must be like for others who didn't have the same stamina or strength in their limbs as her but even hers were hurting so much

from all the standing. She held her hand out towards the woman as if to try and comfort her.

"Maybe she's asleep," she replied, hoping this would help the woman.

"Yes, that's it, that's definitely it," the woman said, nodding her head gently as if to convince herself that was true but crying still.

The dancer, waking up from her short escape through her dream, wanted to cry but held it back thinking she needed to be strong no matter what the outcome was going to be. She squeezed her lover tight.

"You okay?" he asked.

"That's an understatement," responded the theatre owner, near enough to hear it, speaking in a very patronising way.

"Stop it," responded the theatre director. "It's just a term that someone asks if they are concerned about someone so don't be mean."

"That's rich," he replied. We were all told when we were put in that special place that we were all safe and would be free to leave at some point and now we are off to a camp and god knows what's going to happen to us there.,I'm not being mean just realistic."

"Well you just need to stop. We are all trying to cope and survive but then again you always thought yourself above everyone else."

"Now that is mean," replied the owner.

"Yes you're right, I'm sorry," responded the director.

Hugging his lifelong friend, he said, "Forgive me, please."

"Yes of course, my fault too and a really bad trait of mine to undermine others' feelings. I have often thought about it and decided it's due to my very strict and emotionless upbringing, I feel."

"Very sad," replied the director, "but you can change that, you know."

"And now would be a good time you think, and why?" replied the manager in a very defensive, almost sarcastic way.

"Especially now," said the director and he blew a kiss to the dancer and her lover. They smiled back, knowing that this interaction was normal for their two very good friends and under different circumstances would have fuelled the conversation for fun. But not this time.

"Don't do that," responded the owner to the director, "you'll set her off again," he smiled and blew a kiss in her direction himself, "but we love her for that."

She couldn't even remember the last time she ate and just at that moment the baker and the cleaner struck up a conversation about breakfast. People responded by telling them to shut up and did they have no feelings about others? The dancer called out, "Please, let us dream, let's remember what it's like to be human, please go on."

The director and manager looked at each other in a knowing way and approved of her response wholeheartedly.

The dancer listened to their conversation and was taken back to the main street, back outside in the sunshine sitting at a little round metal table with a tablecloth on it that didn't quite cover it but looked pretty anyway. Having a coffee and breakfast with a friend, colleague, lover, brother, sister was just simply that. She smiled as she heard them do the usual, "Hello my dear, a coffee?"

"Oh yes please, and a croissant, chocolate, I feel extravagant."

"What's new today?" the cleaner laughed a little as her own comment had amused her but then very quickly stopped as she knew some couldn't engage in the same way and wanted to respect their feelings.

"No no, my dear, they can't take our memories too, so we mustn't let them," said the baker.

She understood completely what he meant but survival meant different things to different people. That's if survival was what you were destined for?

How did it all come to this, thought the dancer. Trying to recall the story of her life, and also the lives of others. She looked around the carriage and tried to look at as many faces as she could, as though they would then be saved forever as a memory of their lives, who they were, those they loved, of now, and never forgotten no matter what.

She was then overwhelmed by this self-allocated task and began to weep a little but wiped her eyes quickly. "I must be strong, I must be strong," she whispered to herself.

"You okay, my darling?" said her lover.

"Yes, yes, I'm okay," she replied.

She was suddenly struck by the absurdity of the question at this point in time and space, but not in an uncaring and thoughtless way towards her lover. A very nice but almost unrelated question that would make more sense might be, "Are you feeling angry, upset, abandoned, hurt, frightened?" and the list could go on, but we never do ask that, do we? We just carry on with everything no matter what, accept our lot, never revealing our true feelings, never saying enough is enough. She had really got herself worked up now and must have been expressing this physically through her body, muscles and bones because she suddenly felt a little wobbly and her lover noticed, as he would, as they were packed so tight that every little movement was felt. He said nothing, just held her tight to him and kissed her forehead. Sometimes she wasn't sure if he understood her and really who she was and then at moments like this she knew he did.

She wondered how long they had been in the carriage? Most of the time they were moving with just one stop, to push more people into the already overcrowded carriages. Then you could hear the commanding voices outside. Full of confidence. Power exuding from every word, every breath shouting commands to the so-called powerless beings, not even caring if they understood or not, if they live or die or how they die. Why was the how suddenly so important to her? Not me, she thought to herself, not me.

It had been at least one whole day and a night?

"How long have we been in here?" she asked her lover.

"Nearly three days I think, my sweet," responded the director.

"It feels like so much longer," she replied.

"It certainly does," he responded. "If only we could see you dance that would make it so much more bearable. I don't think you realise how captivating and emotive watching you is, my lovely one."

"That's for sure," replied the manager.

She thought for a very short moment and then started to sing, a tune they were very familiar with. The director joined in with her.

She raised her arms slowly, the pain was so strong, but she continued until they were visible to almost everyone. Her lover held her as he had often wished he could when she danced. She held them erect as if waiting on stage for the late arrivals to sit and for all eyes to be on her, waiting for the performance to start. Her long arms bathed in the sunlight that was stabbing its way through the slats of the wooden carriage as they began to move; they were dancing, and it was beautiful. Everyone looked up in her direction, transfixed as though they were also a part of the performance they watched as the story unfolded, and she felt alive.

The train came to an abrupt stop. Everyone took a breath and then panic set in. This felt like the destination. You could hear so much noise through their wooden cage, shouting as truck doors were being opened and the inhabitants

dragged out, forced out at gun point, dogs barking, people crying, begging for mercy and some just in complete shock.

The dancer looked at her lover, her eyes wide open. She grabbed him tightly and kissed his face many times, repeating, "I love you, I love you, I love you," as though this may be the last time she could tell him.

She glanced over quickly at the director, also her very good friend, tears in her eyes. "I love you too, my dear," he said as he gazed back at her with such understanding in his gaze. Comforting her even now.

The doors of their carriage were flung open, it was cold, but the sun raced in in all its glory, determined to shine no matter what. The people of the truck all simultaneously put their hands up to shield their eyes and, as if they were finishing the performance she had started, she drew her arms and hands down slowly. The performance had been ended. The curtains of the stage not completely closed, and the immediate horror not fully comprehended but about to reveal itself.

Chapter 3

A WARM BED

The dancer and her lover were dragged off the train along with the others.

They clung desperately to each other, so so tightly that it almost hurt.

There were guns pointing at them, what looked like random queues of people, people wandering, looking so bewildered, angry, upset, confused, bleeding, desperate.

The men and women in uniforms were shouting orders, again not even caring if their words were understood; those who questioned their orders were beaten or shot. Herding human beings as though they were animals, no – much less than animals.

She felt like she was in some kind of semi-conscious state, not quite being able to believe or her brain not wanting to accept what she saw and heard.

It felt like every fight for life was on a knife edge.

Suddenly, she felt her lover being pulled away from her.

"No," she screamed, "No, no, no." He looked at her and shouted, "Don't worry my darling, don't worry." She wanted to shout back, "Don't be so fucking stupid," both not wanting to accept that this may be the last time they see or hold each other.

But she knew that there was nothing at all he could really say to make this any easier or better and that his words really meant "I will always be with you".

She was being dragged by her feet, not even feeling like they were moving willingly but being pushed towards a queue of females, holding each other, looking so terrified. They were being herded towards the front of a big tall building, but she couldn't be sure because she felt quite faint now and things were looking and feeling quite blurry. This sometimes happened to her when she felt really stressed or anxious about anything, except her dancing. Some, like the theatre owner, would often tease her about her delicate nature.

She looked around to try and see if she could locate her lover, the director, anyone she knew, and she was almost positive she could hear music!!!

She caught a glimpse of her lover and shouted across, he turned just in time to see her and wave frantically, blow a kiss and shout, "I love you." She shouted it back but then he was gone, but at that moment it was as if every single memory of her life was being stolen, and the fight was to remember as much as possible.

Her mind drifted back in time to a day a few days before. Maybe the thought of never seeing her lover again brought it to the front of her mind.

Ah, that's why, they were in bed, wanting that warmth and closeness. It was morning, she can't remember which day as by then they had all merged. A bit chilly but sunny and they were cuddling close to keep warm. It wasn't their home but a place they were brought to with others and told it was safe, away from the streets, the poverty, hunger, smell, degradation, absolute desperation and death.

They felt like they had a chance to survive, to live. For the first time in a long time they could smile. Revel almost in being able to be themselves.

She had always been struck by the fact that he had stood by her all this time even though he was not like her. He could have had a very different life away from all this violence and horror. He wasn't on any unwanted list; he could have had a normal life, marriage, children, boring job.

"What are you thinking?" he said.

"You know me so well," she giggled.

"I think I'm feeling grateful at this moment," and she gave him an extra big hug. "But also still sad about how we got here and where we will end up."

"It will all be okay, my sweet."

"But how do you know?"

He sighed as though he knew there weren't really any reassurances he could give, but couldn't face having this conversation at this moment.

"Why sigh?" she asked.

"Can we just enjoy the moment?"

"We can still enjoy it even if we discuss some of the other things, no?"

He went quiet and then so did she but not for long.

"You could've been safe; you could've had a different life," she blurted out.

"This again," he replied in a fatigued manner.

"Why do you always make me feel like this?"

"Like what?" he said, not realising he had now been hooked.

"Like how incredible I think it is that you have stayed with me through all of this when you could've walked away and been safe and lived a life."

"Because I love you and everything about you, you pain in the arse," he laughed and she joined him.

"No seriously, why?" she said.

He knew what she meant and realised at this point he needed to explain more.

He was quiet for a while trying to think about how he could put it so she would understand what this meant to him.

He sat up slightly and so she did the same, but her hair was sticking out on one side and he giggled. "What?" she said. He pointed and looked a bit sheepish but giggled again.

"Oh," she said and brushed her hand down across her hair to flatten it out and smiled." "Better," he nodded.

"Well, still waiting," she said.

"Yes, I know but I'm trying to think of the words," he replied.

"Well, for a writer you're not doing very well." They both giggled.

"That's it, I think," he said, "even though our destinies could've been very different because of who we are and who we were born to, it's like we were destined to be together, brought together even. Our love was always meant to be because that's how the world and human beings are."

"I thought you didn't believe in god, destiny or faith."

"I don't and that's not what I meant," he replied.

"It's like love is not just the emotions and feelings that people have for each other but their ability to love no matter who, or despite everything, everything that is happening and the consequences. That is our freedom and I suppose for me I am willing to fight for that and not run away."

She was quiet, overcome with emotion.

"That's beautiful," she replied.

"Oh, don't cry, my darling," and he smiled, and he knew if the director saw this moment he would say, "Is she off again, hahaha?"

They cuddled in silence for a while.

"But why is this all even happening, why do we even have to go through this," she cried.

"It's so complicated, I feel," he said.

"No, it's not, it's just hate, pure and simple."

"It can't just be hating."

"What is it then? Because whatever it is it's human beings doing this to other human beings!!!"

"Exactly," he said.

"I don't understand," and she looked up at him and pulled a funny face.

"You're so beautiful," he said.

"No, you don't get off that lightly." she smiled, "but compliment accepted."

"I think it is exactly because we are human beings and have the ability to shape the world around us and, and, and er…"

"No, carry on, I think I'm getting to kind of understand what you mean so carry on."

"It's not that we are just animals but all of that gets mixed up with our feelings, anxieties, hopes and fears and…" she interrupts him.

"So these monsters are doing this because they are a little upset about something," she says in a voice that's a little confused and almost angry and before he could respond, "It almost sounds like you're saying we have to come to an understanding and almost pity them."

"No, no my darling not at all, that's absolutely not what I'm saying at all."

"I'm just like you, totally in shock and horror and disbelief at what is happening."

"But you're not like me though, are you?" she replied.

The lover jumped up out of the bed. "Oh my god, you're not saying what I think you are, are you?" He was almost shouting now.

She looked over at him and shrugged her shoulders.

He froze naked, standing, his eyes filling with tears. Looking directly at her.

"I'm not excusing them if that's what you're implying, that I'm likely to because I'm one of them and not one of you and anyway what does one of them even mean?"

She sat up and put her hand out to him. "No, I'm not saying that, or am I, I don't know, I just don't know." Her hand still stretched out towards him beckoning him back.

He turned away towards the old dusty, broken down dressing table and grabbed for a cigarette. He lit up and took a deep breath and sighed. She could see he was trying to find something to say to either dispel her myth or change the subject. But he remained uncharacteristically silent.

It moved her deeply to see him so upset and she realised at this moment how much she truly loves him. But in all her fragility and delicateness she was stubborn to the core. It was as if both were having a silent row with the air around them, in their own heads, which one would break first?

Suddenly the dancer is back at the camp. The noise is almost deafening. She feels in deep, deep shock. Are these the last moments of her life, she thinks? At that moment she stops, stops to listen. It's true there is music. "There is music," she says out loud as though it has been sent to save her. She looks around frantically, her ears almost leading the way, taking on a life of their own. She must find it, hear it, it must mean something. The group she is huddled with are moved on with brute force and violence but at that moment she hears it, violins and cellos; she knows what piece it is, she thinks, she's danced to it many times. She suddenly takes stock of herself; maybe she is imagining it. Making it up to try and deal with everything that's happening.

"Aaahhhh," she gasps aloud as they draw nearer to the big building. "It really is, it really is, oh my god," she says to herself as though she's discovered something that no one else knows exists, like you do when you are a child and, in your exploration, you discover something you feel needs to be kept a secret. There is a group of musicians playing.

She looks around in disbelief, looking to see the reactions of those in uniforms, in charge, the ones with all the power, but they either can't see it, or they know but just don't care.

Then in a panic she looks for her lover; she has to tell him. She can't see him and is filled with despair and sadness. Desperately wanting to tell him that she understood what he was saying about loving her and not being like the monsters. She starts pushing, trying to free herself from the group. It's impossible. All the time the music is playing, she looks up at the sky, the clouds, the sun and it's all the same, the same as every day, it doesn't change apart from the seasons; it just does what it does every year and watches,

watches what's going on, neither accepting nor disbelieving but never intentionally intervening.

The dancer hears the music again and it's very close now and she listens as though it's just for her; it's beautiful, truly beautiful and surrounded by all this ugly horror. Her group is stopped by the uniforms. They are separated into different groups; why, she asks herself, could there still be hope? The music makes her feelings stronger. Suddenly the will to survive beats in her heart so powerfully she is almost overwhelmed by it. At that moment as she is still and thoughtful, she is suddenly alone, alone on the stage and she begins to raise her arms. Now she is confronted by one of the uniforms who has recognised her, grabs her and drags her nearer to the big building and stops before a very important looking uniform, a general maybe. He is sitting down and looks smug, disinterested in anything that is happening in front of his eyes. As though it's all a bit of an inconvenience.

He looks in her direction and smiles. She can't help it, she smiles back but doesn't know why she did, maybe habit? She feels bad as she didn't mean to smile back, how awful she did that, she thinks. The uniform excitedly talks to the general, yes let's call him that. He gestures in a way that looks like dancing.

She looks around in a bewildered state, still looking for her lover, the director, even the woman in the carriage, someone, anyone.

The uniform gestures towards her, shaking her arm in a way that implies she should know what he's talking about. He points to the musicians and waves his arms about. Now other uniforms join in and acknowledge her. They start smiling and gesturing towards her too. She thinks she understands now.

They want her to dance.

Chapter 4

DAY TO DAY. CENTURY TO CENTURY

Booba at this moment must stop typing. It all feels a little too real and as she knows what's coming, she starts to feel quite emotional. A cup of tea, yes. People often say there is a thin line between love and hate but Booba thinks differently. Rubbish, yes, emotion is a big part of what makes us who we are but not the whole part, no? She can remember emotions that led her to do and say things she now regrets but they were of the moment, it doesn't make them excusable at all, no, not a bit but maybe a little more understandable. Is that what the dancer and her lover were trying to grapple with? No, she thinks there's definitely more to it than that.

There has to be more thought to it all, of course there is. People don't just wake up and say I know, let's have a war, let's enslave or slaughter millions of people just because we feel a bit emotional today. There's the planning. Booba feels a shiver as she thinks about what that actually means. A decision is made

and then the planning, the planning, maybe around a big table in a board room, somewhere they discussed it like it was a shopping list. When is the cost of anything worth that? She's off again she feels, and smiles to herself.

She thinks about her little bubelas, imagines what amazing, strong and beautiful females they are going to grow up to be and how their passion and courage could change the way things are, yes there's always hope.

She smiles, can't quite believe she's a booba, where has the time gone?

Does it go by faster when you feel more optimistic or slower, she can't quite decide?

When, as humanity, did we become stripped of our ability to care about others? Or experience something that gives us that hope? She guesses it can all happen simultaneously, well let's face it, it does, so the answer is both. It becomes a struggle between the two.

Chapter 5

THEY'RE HERE WITH US

Her lover turns and grabs his clothes from a chair and starts to get dressed; still they remain in silence.

She jumps up out of bed and grabs his arm, affectionately but strongly. "Please my love."

He turns away as tears fall down his cheek, he's still upset about what she said to him. Her doubt of his sincerity, his love for her is almost too much to bear.

She turns his head with her hand gently and looks him in the eyes. He looks back and grabs her body so hard; they embrace.

"I'm going to the hall," he says and leaves the room.

She stands there a bit dazed, emotional. "No, no, no, I'm not going to let them do this to us," she says aloud. She grabs her clothes and dresses quickly, no time to lose, literally.

She stops to look out of the window and sees the uniforms with all their guns, standing around, laughing, so confident in their position, power. She pretends she has a gun and aims at them but even in its pretence she can't bring herself to do it.

She looks around at the room, dirty, broken. What was this place before they were all brought here? It could have been a hotel, a rather cheap one, she thinks and smiles cheekily to herself. Maybe even a barracks, an old factory. But at least for now they are together, safe?

She finishes dressing and combs her hair with an old broken comb, but it still makes her feel better and she makes her way downstairs to the hall.

The hall is a biggish room with a few tables and chairs again, dirty, dusty and shambolic. But it's a space where they can all meet up and feel a little more normal, shake hands, hold hands, reminisce, tell stories and just be themselves for a time.

There is lots of chatter and even some laughter. Her lover is at a table with the director and theatre owner and a few other people she has seen but never met properly. She joins them and they all introduce each other, very politely, like the old days and it does make her smile.

The director goes to a bigger table and brings them all some glasses and a jug of water; he's like that, so caring and thoughtful. She sits next to her lover and squeezes his hand under the table, he looks at her and leans over and kisses her cheek.

They are all sitting now and there's a short moment of silence. A woman who introduced herself as the actress blurts out, "Goodness me, I'm so hungry."

They all react politely and giggle.

"Yes," replies the prop maker, "what I wouldn't give for some warm bread and butter."

"Yes," replies the set designer, "and maybe some hearty warm stew."

They all agree and pretend to start eating this most delicious feast.

"Some red wine wouldn't go amiss," retorts the theatre owner.

They all stop eating their imaginary feast and lift a glass to each other and drink the water and make a toast as though it was a lovely Bordeaux.

"They can't stop us remembering," the director says, and they all raise their glasses again.

He starts humming a tune and they all close their eyes and let themselves be absorbed into the notes, the dancer joins in and their voices are very pleasant together, not perfect but that was the point.

The director and the dancer both stop, and they all turn towards the other side of the hall as a singer begins to sing and it's breathtaking, beautiful, accompanied by a musician who has the only piece of musical equipment in this prison-like space. They perform together and it is captivating. They could for a while be somewhere else, someone else. Back in the theatre maybe? Tears well up in the dancer's eyes. She wishes she could get up and dance, but she is frozen, frightened even.

"Go on," says the theatre owner, gesturing towards her.

"I can't, I can't, I, I, I…"

"Please don't," says her lover, "she's very faint."

"Yes, leave the poor girl alone," says the director. "I don't like this tune anyway," and he folds his arms affirming his opinion.

"Why?" responds the dancer, "I think it's gorgeous."

"I just can't bring myself to like something written by someone so horrible in their views of others."

The dancer thinks she understands but surely it is just music. Before she has a chance to respond he continues.

"It's not like the music itself is hateful but we have to make a stand sometime, surely, and to think of it, it does change the way I listen to it and the notes are sometimes structured in a particular way, always following an accepted pattern."

"That's ridiculous," responds the theatre owner.

"No, I do understand," she says, "it can make you interpret it differently."

"Yes, yes that's exactly what I mean."

"But sometimes the beauty of its timing and elegance of the placing of the notes is something that can be appreciated whoever wrote it. Imagine if you didn't know who wrote it, how would it be then?"

"I don't disagree, my angel, but the problem for me is when I do know I can't unknow. It affects me deeply and then I want everyone else to know."

"So, they should stop listening to it, reading it, seeing it in a gallery. Deny that it's a part of our history?" she asks.

"Whose history? And YES, absolutely," he replies.

"That's just denial," exclaims the theatre owner.

"Can we not just accept it for its beauty?" says the lover.

"They can't stop us doing that and, in fact, is that not an act of opposition itself?" she adds.

They all nod and frown at the same time, not sure if they agree with her but acknowledging that it was a very good point.

"The issue for me is…" blurts the director.

They all look at him in a slightly disapproving way as though they thought the discussion had ended, and on such a profound point.

"No, hear me out please and if I can't express this now at this moment in time, in this space, with you all, then when?" He is visibly distressed and upset, which is very unusual for him and more so because he was demanding their attention which, again, he very rarely did. Even as a director he was always very patient and always listened.

They turn to him respectfully and openly, waiting for him to speak. He deserves that at least.

"Art in all its forms does deserve to be understood and appreciated on every level no matter who it is and where it comes from, right, but we know that doesn't happen."

"Not sure what you mean," responds the dancer and they are all now very intrigued.

"What I mean is that not everyone who has the flair or ability to create will get recognised for their skill. Look how long it takes for any artist to achieve greatness and even more so if they are poor and that's if they even do get acknowledged. Imagine how many incredible artists there are out there who will never be discovered or get the chance to have their art seen, heard or appreciated or even have the time or energy to create after labouring for 14 hours. It breaks my heart, and then someone like him comes along and writes a nice tune," he says in a mocking and patronising way. "It makes me so angry."

"But some have written for and about people like us and they have done so meaningfully and truthfully," she replies, "and we can't and shouldn't throw it out as though it doesn't mean anything, surely."

"Where are they now, my darling, where?" he asks.

"They're here, right here with us now," she replies in a triumphant way as she gestures towards her lover.

They all take a breath and look at him not in a new way but almost a redefining way, they always knew but it never seemed to matter but now it's true and they acknowledge it.

The director places his hand on the lover's shoulder and squeezes it hard but with love. He looks back, slightly embarrassed but feeling as though this is the most amazing accolade he has ever received. He goes to respond but feels that no words could sum this moment up.

"Lost your tongue, writer?" the theatre director shouts. They all laugh a little too much. Almost out of relief.

The dancer hugs her lover tight and they all comment and smile at the lovers embracing.

"Share some of that," says the actress.

They all stand up together. The uniforms suddenly turn their gaze to that table and raise their guns. Looking excited at the prospect of a rebellion that they can smash to pieces?

The dancer, lover, director, actress, theatre owner, set designer, prop maker all lean across the table; no rebellion, just a simple embrace, together.

The group sit down again as the uniforms come across and push them back in their seats.

"Why are we here?" says the dancer to the group.

"Oh, please my dear, not that again," replies the lover.

"It's not that, I mean why are we in this place, now?"

"It's because we are creators," responds the director.

They all look at him a little confused.

"Explain," asks the theatre owner.

"We are the window to the world; we create what we see and yes, maybe reinterpret or even question what others have seen."

"So, we are the opposition," the theatre owner retorts as though he's never questioned anything or anyone and he's not happy with that label.

"Not really, although I would be happy to be," replies the director.

"You mean that because we in particular create or interpret in our way we are then rebels for doing that?" asks the set designer.

"Yes, that," replies the director.

"I very much like that," says the set designer.

"Ha, when have your sets ever been rebellious?" laughed the theatre owner.

The set designer looks across at the theatre owner in an indignant way, gets up, excuses himself politely and goes over to the window.

"Because he has created them," says the director, "and don't mock what you don't understand. It's even more important now, go over to him and apologise, now man."

The theatre owner leaves the table and goes to the set designer and they can all see it's quite amicable, thankfully.

They are all very surprised at this new more assertive director and quite like it.

The dancer leans across to the director and squeezes his hand in acknowledgment of his assertion.

"Doesn't mean I agree with you entirely though," and she laughs. He smiles back at her with such a powerful gaze it's like he can read her mind and tells her that for as long as he can he will always be there to reassure her.

At that moment the uniforms suddenly start to run around giving orders. The sound of vehicles outside and lots of noise shake the building as the uniforms start to gesture to everyone.

"I think we are leaving," says the singer.

"Grab what you can, it's cold, very cold," says the director.

They all run back to their rooms and get their belongings, however diminished they are. No one utters a word even if it could be heard amongst all the shouting, loud shouting of the uniforms.

They are all shoved onto trucks, the dancer holding tight to her lover as though their skin was connected by tiny threads, but still looking out for the director.

Both the director and theatre owner are put on the same truck.

"I hope she'll be okay," says the theatre owner to the director about the singer, both looking so sad.

The dancer looks around frantically for the singer, now feeling she needs to locate her even just for her friend's sake, but she can't see her anywhere.

They sit silently in the truck. No one wanting to speak first but all contemplating where this next journey will be taking them.

Chapter 6

A BARREN PLACE

Booba now thinks about how amazing it is that in the face of the most wretched hate, violence and oppression there can still be so much love.

That what makes us human is all we can cling to sometimes.

Their conversation about art really intrigues her though. Our ability to create such beauty, statements of our love or hate for each other. Our confusion, anger at the world. Our complete astonishment at what we are capable of or acceptance that because it exists, that's how it is and how it should be forever? There is so much, and how on earth do we decipher it? Is it just face value, the colour is nice, the sound is pleasant, the movement is moving. Maybe the art is in the act of creating it, not necessarily the final piece, no, that doesn't make sense – or does it?

But the story of the creator is important too, no? Sometimes that is as powerful, good or bad. Or then who exhibits, performs or shows it and how and why is also meaningful. Like the singer in the prison-like place they all find themselves in, singing the song, and the musician playing it; does that redefine it? Booba wishes at this moment she knew more about it all. Feeling she is somewhere in the middle of the debate, again in the middle, she smiles. The only thing she really does know for sure is that the world would be such a barren, cold and boring place without it all.

Chapter 7

PLEASE TAKE
YOUR SEATS

The dancer stands there and looks at the general intensely, not meaning to do so but in contemplation. He sits there looking strong, healthy and happy, yes, happy with his position in life. He smiles, laughs, claps, jokes, hums and holds his head in such a way that says, in this moment, here and now I am free to do what I wish.

How can any human being be that happy and, yes, almost contented in this space that goes on forever where all there is is pain, despair and death?

What kind of person can he be; is he a real person, she thinks? Maybe he'd had a hard life, suffered a great loss? But surely if that were the case that would and should make you more understanding of others and their pain and day-to-day struggle? Not lash out like a child that's fallen and hurt themselves and wants to share the pain even if just for a brief second. Even now she is trying to rationalise what she sees as though finding the truth will somehow make things more bearable. Her childhood was hard too, impoverished, losing her parents at such a young age but, like so many in her community, suffering was something you almost lived with like a relative of life itself; you got used to it. You didn't or tried not to let it affect how you treated others. Well, most did anyway. Surely, that's the most important or significant sign of being a stronger, better person?

She then remembers the argument, no, conversation, no, argument that she had with her lover on this very topic. She can't decide but argument sounds so final she doesn't want to give it that label. That maybe she understands now why he tried to understand why, and it wasn't that he was being too generous to such monsters but more a way of trying to come to terms with it all? It was one of their first arguments; they generally got on so well, very well. Even though he was a little shy at times he did try really hard to be affectionate and engaging around others and she appreciated that but never told him she did, but he did nonetheless and she needs to tell him she knew how hard it was for him. She looks around desperately for a moment to try and find him again. There are too many people and the uniforms are growing restless with her delay to the proceedings.

She is so alone, the space around her has grown and lots of uniforms are shouting towards her, at her and gesturing. The general also gestures but in an almost nice, encouraging, generous way. As though it's a choice she has. He looks at her as though he desires her but is disappointed in himself for those feelings, which makes her even more confused but also angry.

She looks around almost frantically for an audience that would justify this act; not this audience, they/he don't deserve it, but the uniforms are now getting angry with her as the general's smile is beginning to wane. She's being disobedient and now he's not happy. My choice, she thinks, we'll see.

She hears a voice, one she recognises, "Dance, my darling." It's the director.

"Dance, my beauty, for me," he shouts from another area, fighting his way through the tightly knit lines and groups of people so she can see him. He knows if she doesn't, she will almost certainly be shot right there. He couldn't bear that.

Tears well up in her eyes as she frantically spins around and tries to locate his whereabouts. She sees him. She breathes deeply, crying but smiling at him, clinging onto anything that feels like a life she once knew. She wipes the tears from her face, smudging the dirt into her skin.

Its almost as though her reason to dance has now appeared; she will dance but it's especially for him, her friend. Her very close and maybe even her longest friend who is now sitting in the most expensive seats in the theatre, not because he must be there but because he has chosen to be. The dancer gathers her thoughts and looks up to the sky, the clouds, the sunshine, the trees, but no birds. There are no birds here, she thinks, even they have left this horrible place or maybe they are hiding like so many others have had to do.

The music starts again, she recognises the tune but can't remember its name, but it is lovely. Would the director approve? Of course, he is always so supportive. She raises her arms and extends her leg. Immediately her torso

looks different, defiant, tall and it's as if she could reach the sky and jump and grab a cloud. She's not sure if this place is the final place, the last place she will ever dance or breathe. If it is then this requires a performance like no other and it is then she decides what her own fate, her own end will be.

The director watches the dancer with amazement and the emotion of their journey together to this point makes him feel overcome. Her beauty, not just physical, but her endless zest for life. Her continuous questioning of the meaning of everything. Also, her relentless clinging to her spirit and love of performing as a statement of who she is and where she is from.

In this moment he finds himself reflecting back to the first place they were all ordered into. It was like a ghetto, a broken part of town. Some of it was streets they knew but almost unrecognisable now that no one else wanted them. They were all driven from their homes by uniforms with guns. To a place where people were packed into tiny spaces with each other, food was sparse, people so thin were begging in the street. People were dying of diseases that not even those skilled to do so could cure as they had no medicines, tools or spaces. Buildings and rooms you could hardly call home that people tried to give warmth to, although even keeping physically warm was hard. Most people tried so hard to maintain normality in the face of such squalor and pain. What else could they do? Children played together, and the dancer would join them and make the director smile. She would teach them to dance and they would all be happy. But even that didn't last for long before shots were fired, and gun butts used if the children expressed their natural urge to question. The streets were familiar, but they weren't the same as they hadn't chosen to live there. They were forced to because of who they were. But still fighting for some semblance of normality, whatever that was, despite the fact it was a life so far from any reality any of them envisaged.

Performers tried so hard to bring smiles and cheer and that was hard but at least it reminded people of what life used to be like and what it is to be a human being, to laugh and cry but at a story that wasn't yours, made up simply for your entertainment.

Some tried to escape, and others tried to get in to see their friends and maybe even get them out but if caught were killed instantly or brutally interrogated and tortured and left in the streets for all to see.

It was a relief, she thought, when they were then taken to the next place, another displacement but each maybe offering hope of a different outcome but not this place, no hope here, she thought.

The director continues to gaze at the dancer. Already the general and other uniforms are staring. Despite her ripped, dirty clothes and body her form is so beautiful it captures your gaze instantly. The music is played by those just like him and the dancer pierces his soul with the most agonising truth of what this place is, realising this was the last time she would dance, which demands his utmost attention. No matter what that would take he would give it and if it was his last abiding memory then so be it.

The dancer looks to the people playing the music, no, not just people, the orchestra and this, her new stage. She looks to the director and smiles, a reassuring smile. He so wishes he could run to her and hold her close, but he can't. She begins to move, gliding gently in the space now dedicated to her performance. The uniforms are almost frozen in time as is the general who is now sitting forward, mesmerised.

She is very tired and hungry and can feel her body saying, "I'm not sure I can do it," but she now knows she must. Her blood pumps through her body fast as though sending a message to her muscles to keep going, be strong, you can do this. She now moves as though she were the wind itself, telling everyone what it had seen on its journey around the world. She just for a second wobbles, the hunger is fighting back, the audience doesn't notice as they don't know the dance but what they don't know is that neither does she. Normally she would create a performance and then practise and practise until she knows in her heart that it is ready to be performed in public and not a moment sooner. Never has she danced an unpractised piece but today she is improvising.

The director watches as others are and feels such pride and love for his friend. He thinks about how long he has known her and how their friendship has grown so much over the years and how he was hoping to be by her side at her wedding. After his wife died, he was so heartbroken he vowed never to love again but the love he felt for the dancer came very close, but as a father figure! The endless times she would take him, no, drag him shopping with her, looking for outfits and other trinkets for the big day and now wishes he hadn't made so much fuss about it and just appreciated those moments with her and, yes, told her more often that she was the daughter he always wanted but never had. I hope she knows this, he says to himself, almost getting quite anxious that she should know but how can he tell her now, he can't interrupt her performance.

The music is now pulsing through every single vein and muscle in her body as she moves around the space. It's like she has been taken over by the spirits of all the prisoners in this horrible space. Willing her to shake the very ground she dances on so this is not just for her but for all of them too. The only person missing from the audience is her lover or maybe he is there, but she just can't see him. He used to do that. Pretend he wasn't there and hadn't seen her perform a new dance. He would meet her in her dressing room and ask her how her performance had been, and she would reply in a way suggesting she didn't care he hadn't been there but really did. "Of course I was there, you silly thing," he would say. "As if I would miss it for the world and it was beautiful just like you, my darling." Then everything was okay, and she could smile and hug him. So, in her heart she knew he was there watching.

With every swerve of her body towards the general's direction she looks him up and down, very closely. He looks back and around at his uniforms in an arrogant way as if to say, "Look at her, even she can't resist me." They all respond with a giggle, a smirk or a nod, knowing exactly what he meant as they had seen it too.

It feels as though she is dancing forever but only seconds have passed and the general gestures he wants more; she could die on her feet amusing him and he wouldn't care. This only fuels her desire to reach the end of the dance.

Her memory suddenly takes her back to the first time she knew that a dancer was what she wanted to be. It was a family party, an occasion in the calendar. She was about nine years old, she recalls. Everyone was chatting, singing, happy, poor but happy. The music always made her feel different. It was like each note would be saying to her blood it's our turn now and it would pulse through her body and reach her heart and she would have to dance. Everyone at the party would encourage her and be astounded by her innate ability to move in such an incredible way. Her father would say, "I'm not an expert but isn't she amazing?" Then a big debate would ensue as to whether a girl from her background could even make a career of it, let alone the costs of such an extravagant move and this argument would always end in a truce but with the call for more dancing.

She was so happy then, but she has been so happy since, despite the loss and hardship. She became a dancer and quite a well-known one at that. She found love and true friendship. So, she thinks, I have lived so if my end is now maybe I've had more than all these uniforms and the general put together. Maybe that's it, it's jealousy, envy? Because no matter what they did to her, her family or her community they always survived and tried in their heart of hearts to continue to love, create lives and beauty. Strangely, this gives her a little more determination; she lifts her head even higher and looks straight at the general and begins to move very gently and slowly closer to him.

The director stares and wonders as he has guessed by now that this was an improvisation; very unlike her, he thinks. He wishes he could step into her mind and take every step with her. He knows something is different, but he can't reason why he feels this strange feeling. He has a knot in his stomach. It's not hunger as they haven't eaten for so long that he's almost forgotten what hunger itself feels like. It's like a foreboding. What is going through her mind, he considers? He looks to the man next to him. A much older man, so thin and weak. He has the most incredible eyes, the director thinks to himself, quite taken aback. It's so easy to just see everyone in this place as the same empty lost souls, characterless, dehumanised. He can't help gazing into the man's eyes, they are almost telling his whole life story, still reflecting a yearning for life. He is holding his arm tightly, almost an embrace, he gazes back at the director and speaks in a dialect he cannot understand word for word, but he understands what he is trying to say. She is speaking to everyone through her dance no matter what language they speak. He looks around and sees so many people captivated by her movement and in their eyes hoping such beauty could go on forever and their lives be saved.

The director thinks to himself he has always been an optimist, even during some of the most terrible of times but now it fails him. At what moment was this decided, at what point were we all so fearful that we did nothing? But I didn't do nothing, we didn't do nothing, he tells himself emphatically. I wanted people to watch my plays about those who were brave enough to take a stand. I even attended several protests myself and he remembers one where several of them from the theatre went, except the owner, of course. The dancer and her lover, he recalls, were particularly loud in their opinions of what was happening, even in the bar afterwards they nearly got forcibly removed but all found it amusing in the end. But at what point did we lose this battle for life? Where is the owner? He suddenly realises he has lost him in all the pushing and shoving and is now so desperate to locate his friend, his very long-standing and close friend. Will he ever see him again, that grumpy old fool? And he begins to sob so much his whole body shakes. The theatre owner never questioned anything in his life and at times even offered excuses as to why this spiteful government made the decisions they made. He remembers fondly some of their drunken evenings, just him and the theatre owner. Both sharing some of their innermost secrets and experiences. This was when he learnt why the owner had never loved or married a woman. The owner knew and trusted the director with this information, and it made him proud that his friend did this. Now he is overcome with grief in a way he hasn't felt until now. He continues to hold the old man up in an embrace meant for someone known much longer, but this relationship is a lifelong hold of fellow travellers coming to the end of their journey. He suddenly looks to the dancer and away from the old man. He thinks he understands her intentions and with every breath he takes he wills her to finish her performance.

Chapter 8

IS IT EVER TOO LATE?

Booba dips her toe in the bath to check the temperature, perfect. She immerses herself in the warm water and puts her head under. Her ears are now closed to most sounds and she wishes sometimes her thoughts could be too. She thinks about the dancer, her lover and her friends, about the places and experiences they have had to endure and feels a little overcome. Is it too late for them, is it too late for everyone? She sits up almost defiantly and splashes her face. "No," she says aloud. It can't and never should be. Pull yourself together, she tells herself.

It's true, we can only live our own lives, but we never do that alone. What she thinks is we all rely on each other for everything, everything, the clothes we wear, food we eat, places we live, music we listen to, books we read, the beautiful creations of others, our conversations, arguments, love and affection and so on, everything, yes everything. Why is this then, the story, the history of us all, divided or decided by a single decision to undermine our basic instinct to share all of this? There is still such amazing beauty in the kindness and understanding we show each other and strangers and solidarity, even in the darkest of all our moments, and that's the truth.

That's why all this is so important to her then, Booba thinks. Because if you don't try to understand then it's like you have accepted it. That it's all just meant to happen like a freak storm or accident but that's not the case is it, she determines as she gets out of the bath and begins to dry herself and go on with her day.

Chapter 9

THE ENCORE

The stage is set, past, present and future and she dances with such commitment it's like she's dancing for all the guests in the theatre, a special performance, maybe someone's birthday or an engagement celebration, something big though. It's like she can even hear all the chatter, laughter and excitement in the voices of those taking their seats and getting ready, full of anticipation for the performance. She would be looking at them from the wings behind the curtain and even she's full of excitement.

She stops for an instant. Is that the voices of children? No, please no, not in this place but as she turns, she sees a small group of children, maybe related or just thrown together like everyone else has been. They are being pulled away from her sight except one of them breaks away and stops to see her dance. They look at each other. The dancer is taken over with emotion, she turns away as she continues to dance, she must finish the performance and the child has just given her even more reason to get to the end. She looks back but the boy is gone. She wishes she could have told him that it was going to be all right or maybe she just imagined them there?

She always wanted children; she reminds herself. Her friend the director used to say she was a child herself and he didn't just mean in years. He also meant in her behaviour too. "A bloody petulant child," he would say and storm out and look back just in time to see and hear the group of friends giggle to each other. "Bloody children, the whole lot of you." But they all knew he loved them. "Oh, come back," they would shout, "please," and then a couple of them would run after him, including the dancer. What she would give to be back there now, and she would cherish every single moment.

What do the children make of this world, she thinks. How would their innocent view of the behaviour of the so-called grown-up people destroying each other be interpreted by them? How do they cope with it all and still be children, with all their open-mindedness? Their courage to try something even if it's a bit scary. Inventing things in their heads that haven't been thought of. Their ability to smile and cry all at the same time.

Her dancing has the uniforms and general captivated. She moves to the music as though she is every note, every chord in human form.

Everything seems strangely clear to her now. As she moves so beautifully, she looks at every one of the uniforms, straight into their eyes. Some of them glare back, some look away as though their own guilt can't bear it and some

pretend they are not interested but they fail in this too. The general, seeing this, sits back in his seat again as though to say he is ambivalent, almost as though he has nothing to do with this place and the horrors unfolding in front of his eyes. Of course, he has, he's the leader but he can afford his separation from this moment as he has the last word, the last say, the power.

Her body spins and her arms reach for the sky as her feet lift the dust from the ground, dust she kicks up with every move. It's like a small smoke screen she's created around her, to protect her. But she only needs protecting until the final chord has been played.

The musicians are playing so beautifully and every note, even on the damaged instruments, means so much. Much like all of the people in this place and the other places she has lived in. So many scars, broken bones, dirty ripped clothes and the pain, the emotional and mental pain of being treated like this, like animals. The smell too, it's so overwhelming. No dignity left here, she feels, or is there? To try and survive all of this, is that possible? She hates the uniforms and the general so much but not because they are who they are, that is what they would want, it's because they have chosen this. How, she wonders? How can anyone choose the destruction of others in this way? What means so much more to them – money, land, destroying something you don't understand or maybe even fear?

Then she remembers her lover; he could have been a uniform or even a general, but he chose differently. Like others they knew too. Not only did he not choose to hate but he chose to love and love her and now he's paying such a huge price for this. Maybe she should run and shout and try to find him, tell him it's not too late to save himself. She would understand. But she knows he would never do that. Like many of their friends who chose not to be uniforms. He would rather give up his life, and it's not just about her but all their friends who have come to be like a family – dysfunctional, almost certainly, dishevelled, different from each other and all of them with a story to tell. Each one as remarkable as the first and last.

She suddenly remembers one of the first times she met her lover. It was after a show and they were all having a drink or two in a local bar. He had just started to work with the theatre and was quite shy and beautiful in his own way, she thought. She had seen him a few times around the place but had never had time to stop and do introductions. The theatre owner grabbed her lover's arm and pulled him over to their table and introduced them to each other as though on a secret mission. He went straight up to the director after and they both giggled like silly children, she thought, but smiled to herself. She found out afterwards that they had a bet on, and the owner won. He was more sentimental than the director, that's why he won, thinks the dancer. They sat in silence for a while, until she asked him where he was staying as a start to a conversation and then realised that sounded too forward and she tried very awkwardly to put it right but messed it up, but they both then laughed. Then they got very drunk and danced all night until the sun came up. They walked back to her lodgings along the river front, just talking and arguing too about the world, people and what was going on and that hopefully it would all blow over and be just like a memory of a bad dream. The rest, as they say, is history.

As she glides to the music, through the dust she sees her lover, waiting for her, his hand extended as he gestures to her to join him. She almost runs and remembers she's performing. She stops for just an instant, remembering she must finish this dance but if he joins her how lovely that will be. She grabs his hand gently and they begin to dance in a beautiful union. Each anticipating each other's moves with such precision. How different their life together would have been? Children, yes children and lots of them but she wouldn't have given up dancing, neither of them would have wanted that. His plays would have been performed around the world and their beautiful children would have been so proud of them both. As they of them. Forging their way in a difficult and fractured world but being proud of who they are and their heritage.

The director, still watching the dancer, sees her moving towards something, someone and then the smile on her face and her extended arm, but to who? He then realises and he whispers under his breath, "Oh my darling, you're with him and there's nothing they can do. I love you, I love you, I love you, my dearest." It's as though by saying so it's an act of defiance so he just keeps saying it repeatedly.

She dances but realises that the music will come to a stop soon and she still has more to do. Her legs feel very weak now but her determination to finish this dance is overwhelming, especially now she is dancing with her lover. She asks him, "Why do they insist I dance, and the musicians play, if they hate us so much?"

"Because such beauty and creativity is not owned by them and never will be so they are trying to control it. It's the only way they know how to be. Their priority is something else, not human beings," he replies.

"Be careful, you're starting to sound like the director," and she smiles. He smiles back.

She turns her head slightly away as her body is almost moving now on its own as more dust is in the air. She sees he has gone, her heart is broken but is now beating so fast, so fast.

There's a scuffle somewhere else which suddenly takes the gaze and attention of some of the uniforms and the general, but guns are fired, and the situation dealt with, but the uniforms are now on their guard. What happened, she wonders. Did someone try to run, to escape or even grab a gun or attack a uniform? It must have been something significant as it took a lot of gunfire and shouting. She can't locate her close friend anymore.

The director manages to avoid the scuffle by crouching very low and moving through it like a small wave, finally falling to the ground and managing to move nearer to the dancer. There he can maintain his view of his friend knowing that soon, very soon, it will be the end of her performance. He has decided too. He wants to survive all of this, whatever that means. He is determined that this will not be the end of his life, in this place and at the hands of these people.

She suddenly sees him but her leg slips from under her and she begins to fall to the ground. The director is overcome with fear and worries that the fall will bring her performance to an untimely end. She can't allow this to happen, she must fight to dance but she is so weak, hungry and exhausted. The musicians continue to play, to urge her to carry on. He wills her to get up.

At this moment a young uniform runs over to her and holds out his hand. She accepts his gesture. But as she does all the memories of the past years come flooding back, the marching in the streets, the slogans, the blaming, the graffiti, the raids, the public beatings, the shootings, the bombings, the imprisoning and continuous moving from one horrible barren place to the next. Why does he come to her now to help her, how can he justify that act in the face of so many actions that contradict his? And she accepts because she must continue to dance, making each movement like a part of the choreography.

At this moment an older uniform marches over and with the butt of his gun hits the young uniform across the head. He stares right at her for a minute, looking right into her eyes and she his. Blood begins to flow down his face, and he puts his hand out towards her, falling against her and then onto the ground into a heap on the dust. The older uniform gestures for her to continue to dance. She moves her arms around her like she is some sea creature floating around on the seabed waiting for its moment to rise to the surface. Trying to disguise her intention as she slowly rises.

The director stares with such anticipation and complete wonder. Not realising that she has grabbed his gun. And neither have they.

Chapter 10

NEVER FORGOTTEN

Booba wonders how then, at this moment in time, you sum up a life lived. Is it about one person, a family, a village, a city, a country, a world? Not all of us can or will be remembered. Some of us are lucky, Booba thinks, we have those around us who will never forget a life lived. Who care enough to care about others, even those they have met and those they will never meet. Will the dancer's last dance be forgotten?

If love could be seen, really seen, what would it look like, how would it be among us? Fragile or strong? Questioning or accepting? Faithful or fickle? Would it look like all of us? Booba feels love all the time and wishes it could be something you could hold in your hands, like those who hold guns and weapons, and use it to stop all the hate, violence and death but that's just a stupid romantic notion she realises, meant for romantic comedies and sci-fi movies. But making a stand against such hateful actions, is that not love, sacrificing your freedom or life for it? Surviving such hate takes a conviction that only love can understand. The need to tell everyone and keep reminding them so that we don't make the same mistakes again and again and again. Is that not the point? Do we let them – the ones whose hearts burn with hate – define it? Is that not the point? Who defines what love means, really, who?

Chapter 11

THE FINAL CURTAIN

The dancer slowly but with a purpose continues to move as though the fall was all a part of the whole choreography. Moving on the ground like an injured bird trying to find its wings again. Desperately trying to ignore the fallen uniform and the blood on the dirt and her coat. The general and other uniforms don't seem that bothered either as they shout at her and gesture in a way that she knows means get up, dance now, it's not over and she knows herself it isn't done.

As she rises, she moves with such elegance and meaning, but with even more determination, that the general sits forward and the uniforms are gazing. The director now breathes again as his fear was her fall would mean an end to her dance and her; he just couldn't face that but, in his heart, he knows the dance will be over soon.

Despite her shabby, bruised and broken appearance, he believes she looks more beautiful than ever before. There is a conviction and determination in her face and movement he has never seen. It's not that he doesn't or hasn't acknowledged her incredible ability and beauty, he has always admitted he could watch her dance forever and a day. Did he ever tell her that, he wonders? "I'm sure I did, I hope I did, well she knew it anyway, I hope, I hope." He wants to shout to her to tell her he will miss her so very much and how dear she is to him, but he can't.

She is now on her feet again, her overcoat swinging as she moves, and as the music is coming to an end soon she feels that every little bit of muscle, bone, blood and water in her body is joining together, uniting to give her the strength she needs. She spins and moves delicately towards the general, raises one arm out and gestures towards him, then brings her other arm out from inside her overcoat and aims the gun straight at him and fires. It hits him in the chest. There is now a rush towards her by the uniforms and she spins and shoots another uniform who runs towards her and another. Then more shots are fired at her, her body now covered in holes and blood, but she continues to spin as though defying death itself.

She finally collapses in a heap on the dirt and the director runs to her. He holds her in his arms and cries helplessly. She has killed the general and at least two uniforms but paid for it with her own life.

There is now chaos; this causes many people who are prisoners in this place to take a moment to decide their own fate. Some make a grab at freedom and run, others attack the uniforms and attempt to take their guns. Others remain still, silent, in shock and fear for their lives and just want to live. For a moment the uniforms look visibly shaken and unsure but very soon their firepower overcomes the many and they are back in control with people lying everywhere, dead or injured. They continue to fire randomly at the crowd just to make sure that they have control.

Uniforms now surround her bloodied, lifeless body as though she is some kind of vicious beast. They drag the director away from her and throw him towards the crowd who try to engulf him as though to protect him. His determination to survive now greater than ever before.

The director, now crying silently but helplessly, wonders what her last thoughts might have been. Were they of her life, although short, her theatre family, her own family or the one she never had? He looks around at others and tries to imagine the lives of the other prisoners. Like the dancer it's as though he has to try and bring them, and humanity, back to life by doing so.

A young woman he sees, he imagines maybe she was a dressmaker or a government official or whatever. She was young, happy, with lots of brothers and sisters who she loved spending time with, although the brothers could sometimes be a little annoying and immature. She would enjoy going to the theatre, having dinner at a nice restaurant but it didn't have to be fancy. She was very independent. Like the dancer, a very determined young woman and strong, but had to be because of her background and the attitudes towards her people she would have encountered. Oh, and don't forget about the attitude towards women too, but he thinks she would have been a worthy opponent in any given argument or confrontation. It's like the director feels he needs to survive to tell everyone's stories and make sure they are not forgotten.

The director thinks about what he has witnessed and the world he inhabits at this very moment and wonders how, why? He has always been a thinker though. The dancer always the doer but he loved that so much about her. He remembers how she almost made it a conviction to do an encore only if it was demanded or asked for by those in the stalls. Especially not the ones in the balcony unless she could tell that for them this was an occasion and one that was saved for. She could always tell as they would definitely not behave as though this opportunity was some god- or power-given right but as an exciting new adventure and one they'd never experienced before but were so happy to have. This became an even stronger commitment of hers when the balcony then became inhabited by the uniforms. This infuriated the theatre manager even more who, after her performance, would follow her to her dressing room

shouting and complaining, "You want us to get into trouble, you want us to be closed down?" he would exclaim. She would ignore his outbursts and just go to her room. This wasn't just a decision by her but almost a physical reaction she couldn't control so no point in having a row about it as it was going to happen again anyway. The director now realises that this particular story was always going to end this way for her.

He imagines how different her life could have and should have been. He then remembers an evening they spent together. They had all gone out for a meal after the show and then a few drinks in a little bar that they all loved to frequent. All of them then decided to take their usual walk along the river. It wasn't summer but it wasn't freezing, just a little chilly but he insisted the dancer put on his jacket as he knew she was cold but would never ask for it. All of them chatting loudly, laughing, arguing about nothing but being themselves and just being happy.

The dancer and the director were together at the back of the group. She told him how strongly she felt for her lover and that she wanted to marry him and knew that at some point he would propose and how excited and warm and at peace it made her feel. She definitely wanted children but not just yet as she wanted some time for them both and for herself and her dancing. The director couldn't help imagining how that would be and how he would fit into it and she reassured him that he was Grandpa. This made him smile so hard outside and inside, but he remained restrained. He would almost certainly be called upon to babysit regularly. He imagines this very clearly and it makes him emotional even now in this moment. He would get the children to create plays, poems, art and then perform them for the returning parents and everyone would applaud. He imagines their children full of their parents' determination to make life a happy one despite anything and everything. They would be beautiful because of their amazing heritage and that would be celebrated in a world very different from this.

That's it, he thinks, you can't stop the course of true love. You can discriminate, criminalise and murder innocent people simply because of who they are but you can't stop love. He looks around again at the faces he can see and feels this isn't the end of love at all. This is because of love and the determination to be allowed to love. This will continue even after today, tomorrow and the next day. It will shape the world in future generations. It won't determine his outcome right now, but he knows that there will always be human beings that will challenge this and will see unfamiliar forms of light they will celebrate and know that it is the only way for the world to be and because of this they will survive.

How will human beings come to terms with what they have done? What excuses will they use, what plans will be made to make sure it never happens again or will the greed to own our souls take over again and again, and will even those who bear the scars repeat it?

He refuses to believe this. He remembers the conversation in the hall and how the dancer pointed to her lover when asked about others being a part of their story and now he remembers it wasn't just her lover, there were others and he now wishes he had acknowledged their presence and commitment but it's too late. No, it's not, it never is. What was his name, he can't recall, but he remembers he was a young and rather handsome young man, the head usher, and a good one at that, so gentle, polite and a great problem solver. Tended to flirt but that was also part of his charm. He knows that the uniforms tried to get him to join but he refused and refused so many times. Oh yes, then there was the cleaner. An older woman, beautiful eyes he remembers, quite stern, not really afraid of anyone but the place was always spotless. Word was that she actually joined the resistance. What became of her, the director asks himself.

He now feels he needs to say a prayer, but he is not so inclined. So he begins to sing a song, gently at first. It was one of their favourites and everyone around would always join in whether it was part of a practice or in a bar after a show, it was a thing they all did together.

The uniforms notice what he is doing and acknowledge it as though he is mad, but he sees it as an act of defiance and remembrance as he begins to move towards her again. The uniforms now grab her lifeless body and drag it away, away from him and others. Out of sight as maybe it would lead to more acts of rebellion.

They push him back towards to the crowd, but he continues to sing for the dancer.

Chapter 12

IS IT MY TIME?

Booba looks out of her window to the street below. She wonders for a moment what made the dancer do what she did. Such courage and bravery or, some would say, stupidity and recklessness. No! She doesn't mean that. She means what was it about her that made her do that? She knows that she had a troubled upbringing. Losing loved ones so young and being poor. Also, of a culture not accepted, continually blamed and attacked for everything that was wrong with society. But she had such kindness and love within her too.

Booba now thinks about her crazy, unorthodox and sometimes scary upbringing and childhood. Which certainly meant she, like the dancer, had to grow within herself a very high level of resilience that would unfortunately sometimes reflect in her misconception of boundaries. Is that it? Would she be brave enough to do what the dancer did? Or have we all got that within us but our journey through life either nourishes that seed or buries it deep, so deep we don't even know we have it? Booba knows that there will have been lots of argument in the camp about the dancer's actions but she's not going to think about that. But Booba feels if you want to discuss it further, feel free and she smiles as she knows.

Booba looks up from her laptop. Did the director survive to tell of what had taken place? Or was it the nurse, teacher, doctor, refuse collector, delivery driver, social worker, shop worker, who survived to tell their story and the story of others who lived through such a terrible time? A time where life was just lists of wanted or unwanted, much like balance sheets of income and expenditure, tick versus a cross; who chooses?

Feeling quite emotional now for all the loss in the past, present and the future unless we confront it. Making a stand isn't easy though, is it? She believes that there is always empathy but that's not enough on its own, there has to be some kind of action otherwise empathy is just an idea, no?

Booba remembers one occasion when she was on a bus. A young Muslim woman was standing by the doors. She was heavily pregnant and had a small child in a buggy. There were two white women sitting together, slightly higher up as they were in the back part of the bus. Maybe being physically higher made them feel more confident because they started to abuse the young mother verbally. Saying the most disgusting things about her, her children and her faith. Booba felt so angry that she had to control herself. She looked around and couldn't see anyone else responding. No one but she knew it was fear as they all could hear and see it but were looking out of the window or in their bags as though they had lost something, or continuing with a conversation that was so important it couldn't be stopped or paused.

Booba got up out of her seat and moved so she was right next to the young mother.

"Hello," she said, "how are you today?"

The young mother looked at her with shock as though this was the last thing she expected.

"I'm okay," she replied.

Booba then knelt down and spoke to the child and shook his hand. She then stood up so that the two women could see her more clearly. She stared at them and waited for them to respond and say something to her. But they didn't. They went silent and looked away. Booba stayed on until the two women got off as she didn't want to leave the young mother on her own with them. The bus reached the next stop and the young mother got off and as she did, Booba asked if she would be okay and she replied yes and then thanked her in a way that made Booba feel quite overcome. She then left the bus herself and crossed over the road to get the bus back to her stop, shaking and crying.

Hate isn't just what you see on a bus, it's such a powerful idea. That the media and politicians encourage or even create it, that's why so many feel fearful of confronting it. Booba can't and won't believe we are born to feel or act this way, no never. Do we accept their interpretation of the world or do we make a choice to question it and maybe even try to see another way? Who is it that controls how we feel about others? It's not just preference as in whether you like Marmite or not. It's a choice about how we live and those choices we make or are allowed to make without shaking the very ground we walk on!

The human race has the capacity to love and/or hate and recently we have all seen the love we can show each other in the face of desperation, hardship and death. The kindness people have shown to strangers, but not just that, also understanding how different we are but how important it is in order for our beautiful world to survive and flourish. It's a bit like a piece of art, a book, a poem, a film that we have all enjoyed without ever meeting its creator, but we have become emotionally moved by it or inspired to respond. That's the potential of us all, she feels.

So much to discuss, she smiles, knowing her Mamma would almost certainly say to her, "Taking on too much again, my darling," as she always did too. A trait Mamma almost certainly passed on.

Booba closes her laptop. Now sitting across the table is the dancer. She draws a breath as they both stare across the table at each other.

"I don't want this just to be a sad story," she tells the dancer. "There is so much hope." She thinks about her own children, her grandchildren, her family and friends. How lucky she is to have existed alongside them and how protective she is of that.

Booba looks at her hand on the table and sees so many years of experiences, good, bad, indifferent, but nonetheless an older hand than she was expecting to see.

The dancer places her hand on Booba's. It's warm and gentle but immediately she can see the millions of children across the world. Like a film of all the possibilities playing in her head .

She is now a little fearful of what this means to her. But she summons up the courage to ask the dancer directly.

"Is it my time now?"

They look at each other in silence for what feels like years.

The dancer puts her head slightly to the side and smiles at Booba.

"No, Booba, there's too much left to do."

Lightning Source UK Ltd.
Milton Keynes UK
UKHW011830310522
403794UK00002B/244